D0440443
Bloody Mary

Bloody Mary

contents

BLOOD ✢ 33 The Wheels of Fate
007

BLOOD ✢ 34 Soul Fragment
036

BLOOD ✢ 35 Atonement
073

BLOOD ✢ 36 Mary and "Mary"
117

A Colloquy on the Bedroom: Follow-Up
160

Postscript
161

Eyes & Hair
Has red eyes and red hair—unusual for a vampire. Also has really heavy bags under his eyes!
Thinking
Suicidal. Has lost count of how many times he's tried to die.
Brains
Levelheaded. Decides in a split second if something's useful to him or not.
Face
Used to have a flat, unnatural smile, but since volume 3 he's started getting wrinkles between his brows.
Heart
Superstrong. Won't die even if you drive a stake through it.
Fashion
Loves his hoodie, which comes with cat ears (and a tail). ♥ He also has one with bunny ears that he got from Hasegawa.
Blood
Type AB. He loses strength if his blood is sucked from the nape of his neck—his weak spot.
Cross
One drop of blood on his rosary transforms it into a large staff that can ward off vampires.
Legs
His height—179 cm—makes him good at fleeing the scene.
Legs
Has an amazing ability to jump. Enjoys sitting atop his favorite lamppost at Bashamichi.
BLOODY MARY
ICHIRO ROSARIO DI MARIA
Mary is a vampire who, after living for countless years, can't stop thinking about death. He has spent centuries searching for a priest named Maria to kill him, and he finally finds him. But it turns out he is the wrong Maria.
Still, Mary is convinced that Maria does carry the Blood of Maria and, therefore, is the only one who can kill him. But with the pact in place, Mary remains alive.
Usually vampires have black or white hair and a limited life span, but Mary has red hair and is immortal, making him an oddity in the vampire world.
An 11th-grade student who attends a parochial school in Yokohama. He became a priest to follow in his late father's footsteps. On the outside, he plays a kind priest. But in reality, he's cold, calculating and willing to use anything or anyone (even a vampire!) to protect himself.
Constantly under threat by vampires, he is unable to stay out at night, but then he makes an uneasy pact with the vampire Mary. He promises Mary he will kill him in exchange for his protection until Maria is able to wipe out every vampire on earth. Now Mary serves as his bodyguard and Maria forces Mary to drink his blood.

"MARY"

Mary's twin brother, who went by the name "Mary" when he was human. His reason for becoming a vampire will finally be revealed...! When you find out, you'll no doubt come to love the nonmasochist "Mary" as much as Mary!

ALDILA

Because of his crazy infatuation with Bloody Eye, he offered up his own left eye for her. Clearly, this guy is reckless. Learn more about him on page 162! This volume will explain why Madam Eye needed his left eye in the first place.

BLOODY EYE

Up to now, Lady Hydra has been the most powerful heroine in the story, but now there's a new powerful vampire heroine to deal with. She is "You-know-who" (as referred to by the trio).

HYDRA

Despite her long life, Lady Hydra is surprisingly naive. She has tried to forget the human girl-child whom she was so charmed by and to pursue a new love. But now that same girl (Bloody Eye) is harassing her again.

Even a masochist could understand it A recap of volume 8 in 2-3 minutes!

Mary finally remembers his forgotten past!

▲ A sadist on a rampage

...And yet, his memory was from when he was human and he killed "Mary" (the nonmasochist). This grave revelation weighs on him, and he flees reality, which allows "Mary" to surface in his place.

As for "Mary"... On one hand, it's good that he's finally come forth, but there's something crazed about him! He's become more and more bloodthirsty... "Mary" is bad news!

▲ A masochist crybaby

▲ The girl who totally duped Lady Hydra

Lady Hydra's Situation

A human girl promised her they'd always be together. But she was only manipulating Hydra in order to save herself from an incurable disease! It was "Mary" (the nonmasochist) who saved her broken heart, and ever since then she's only loved "Mary." "I swear I won't let you go!" says Lady Hydra.

And what's up with Maria?!

He broods about all that but is currently determined to get back masochist Mary, who has disappeared.

Bloody Mary is in danger of being a typical "romance story"...!

BLOOD + 33 The Wheels of Fate

400 YEARS AGO, ON THAT DAY, THE WHEELS OF FATE WERE SET IN MOTION...
I WAS EXPECTING A MONSTER.
BUT...
...YOU'RE BEAUTIFUL.
"DIE, VAMPIRE!"
I CAN FEEL HIS WARMTH...
"I WON'T LET SOME VAMPIRE HURT MY CHILD."
"GET AWAY FROM US!
...THROUGH HIS FINGERTIPS.

NO.
MY CHEST HURTS.
NO.
I DON'T WANT TO CRY.
I HATE...
...HUMANS.
UH ...
WHAT DID I DO?

SMACK
...!
DIRTY HUMAN!
DON'T TOUCH ME!
HEY.
IF I WEREN'T HUMAN, WOULD IT BE OKAY FOR ME TO TOUCH YOU?
I CAN'T JUST LEAVE A PRETTY GIRL ALONE WHEN SHE'S CRYING.
DID I OFFEND YOU?

THEN ...
...I'M READY TO STOP BEING HUMAN.
MAKE ME A VAMPIRE.
"I WANT TO BE A VAMPIRE."
YOU TOO ...
YOU'VE COME HERE TO USE ME.
I DON'T TRUST HUMANS.
LOOM

NOT EVER!
I'M NOT GO-ING TO...
...MAKE THE SAME MISTAKE TWICE.
NEVER AGAIN!
Pau
Se

WHY ...
... AREN'T YOU RUN-NING AWAY?
BECAUSE I KNOW YOU DON'T ACTUALLY WANT TO KILL ME.
...!
WHEN YOU FIRST SAW ME, YOU COULD'VE KILLED ME. BUT YOU DIDN'T.
WERE YOU BETRAYED BY THEM?
AND ...
...YOU'RE SAYING "AGAIN"... WHICH TELLS ME YOU'VE MADE A HUMAN A VAMPIRE IN THE PAST.
IS THAT WHY YOU HATE HUMANS?

THEN I PROMISE YOU.
I WON'T BETRAY YOU.
I HAVE TWO WISHES.
IF YOU CAN GRANT ME EITHER ONE...
...I'LL DEVOTE ALL OF MYSELF TO YOU.

IF YOU WANT TO DRINK MY BLOOD, YOU CAN HAVE AS MUCH AS YOU WANT.
IF I'M IN YOUR WAY, YOU CAN KILL ME.
I PROMISE.
"I DON'T NEED YOU ANYMORE."
---WHY---
AND YET---
HUMANS---
---ARE CUNNING AND SELFISH CREATURES.
I MUSTN'T TRUST THEM.

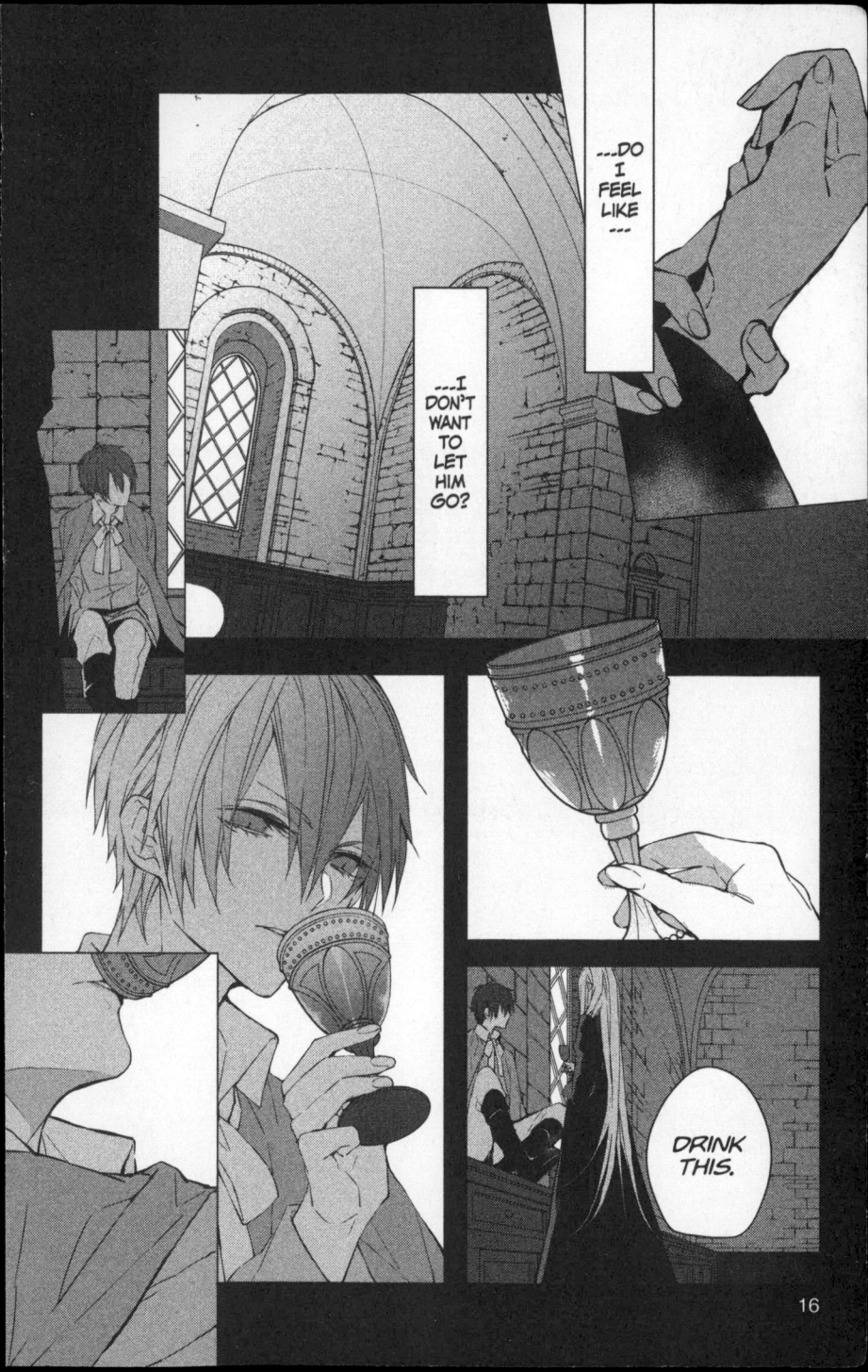
---DO I FEEL LIKE ---
---I DON'T WANT TO LET HIM GO?
DRINK THIS.

THADUMP
THROB!
thadump
thadump
...KUH!
AH...!
W-WHAT WAS IN THERE?
Haah...
haah...!
MY THROAT'S ON FIRE...
THAT WAS MY BLOOD.

YOU HAVE THE MAKINGS FOR IT...
BUT IT WILL STILL TAKE SOME TIME FOR YOU...
AN ORDINARY HUMAN WOULD HAVE DIED INSTANTLY.
...TO BECOME A VAMPIRE.
WE CAN'T DO IT RIGHT NOW...?
Haah...
Haah...
NO... IT'D BE IMPOSSIBLE.
Haah...
rustle
I'M GOING TO MAKE MY SECOND WISH COME TRUE BEFORE HE DIES.
NO...
YOU'RE STILL TOO IMMATURE TO HANDLE MY BLOOD.
Haah...
I'M NOT ABOUT TO DIE.
YOU WOULDN'T WANT TO COME ALL THIS WAY ONLY TO DIE, WOULD YOU?

WHAT'S A KID DOING OUT HERE ---?
I FEEL MARY DEEP WITHIN.
HE'S SOMEWHERE OUT THERE SUFFERING.
MARY... WHERE ARE YOU...

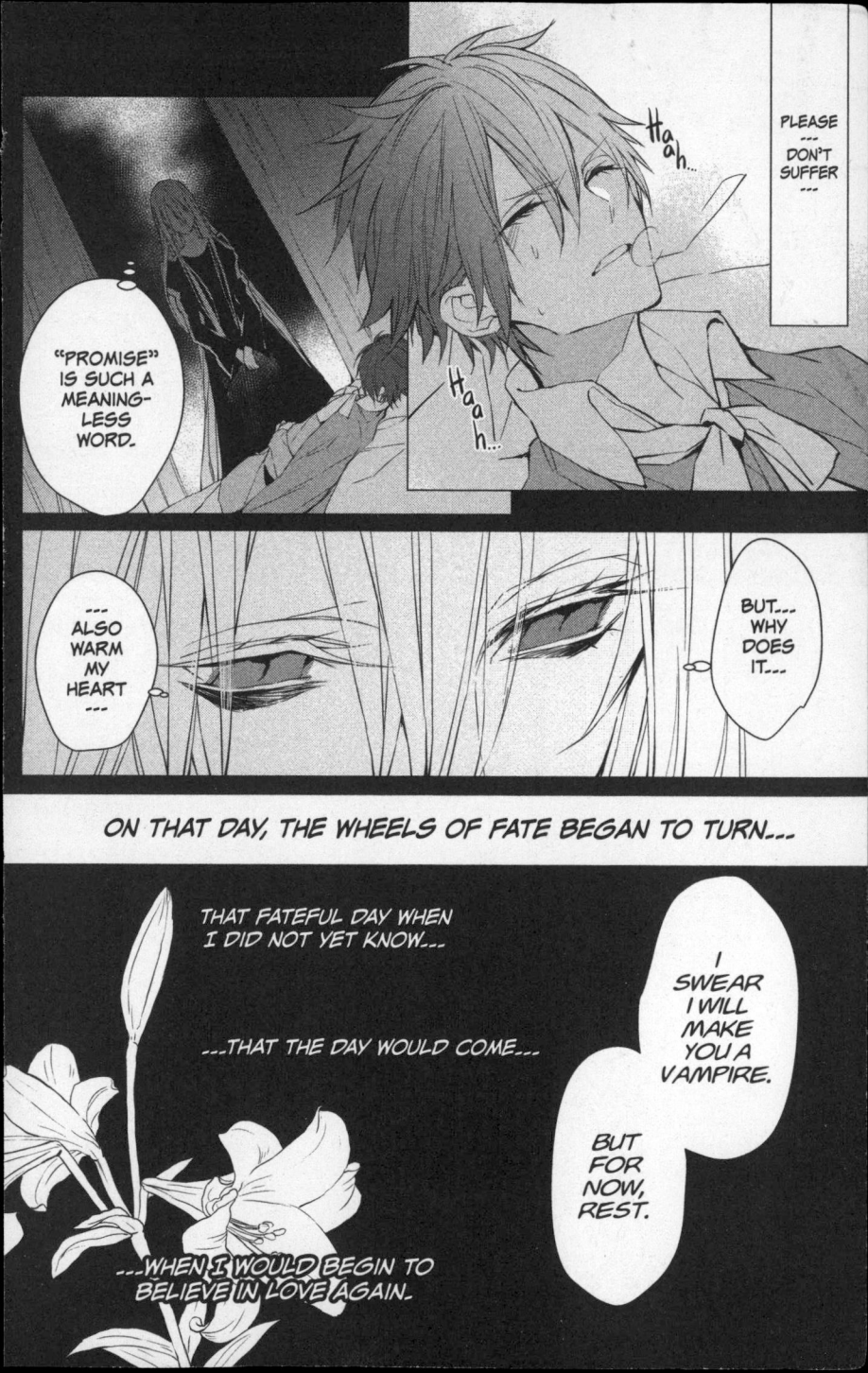
PLEASE --- DON'T SUFFER ---
Haah...
Haah...
"PROMISE" IS SUCH A MEANING-LESS WORD.
BUT... WHY DOES IT...
--- ALSO WARM MY HEART ---
ON THAT DAY, THE WHEELS OF FATE BEGAN TO TURN...
THAT FATEFUL DAY WHEN I DID NOT YET KNOW...
...THAT THE DAY WOULD COME...
I SWEAR I WILL MAKE YOU A VAMPIRE.
BUT FOR NOW, REST.
...WHEN I WOULD BEGIN TO BELIEVE IN LOVE AGAIN.

OUCH.
DON'T LOOK SO SCARY.
tmp
zip
RELAX.
UNLIKE DILA, I'M NOT TWISTED. ♥
IT WON'T HURT. ★

shwf
DIDN'T I TELL YOU?
DON'T TOUCH HIM.

drip
drip
slide
Kah...
YOU... WHY—
HYDRA ...
shwf
THUD
YOU'RE PRETTY STRONG.
I TESTED YOUR POWER.
BUT YOU'RE STILL JUST THAT GIRL'S DOG.
NOT ENOUGH.

YOU KNOW NOTHING ABOUT HER!
DON'T BAD-MOUTH MADAM EYE.
WRONG.
I'M THE ONE WHO CREATED BLOODY EYE.
SO I'LL TELL YOU.
YOU'RE THE ONE WHO KNOWS NOTHING.
THE BLOODY EYE YOU KNEW IS NO LONGER.

BLOODY EYE WAS UNABLE TO HANDLE ALL OF MY BLOOD.
AND SO SHE BECAME AN INCOMPLETE VAMPIRE.
A VAMPIRE AT MAXIMUM STRENGTH WILL STOP AGING.
BUT NOT SO FOR BLOODY EYE.
Heh.
WHAT DO YOU MEAN?
NO LONGER...?
BLOODY EYE NO LONGER HAS THE POWER SHE ONCE DID.
EVEN THOUGH SHE IS A VAMPIRE, HER BODY IS WEAK.

I WONDER WHAT SHE LOOKS LIKE NOW.
SHE'S A DEFECTIVE VAMPIRE.
HA... HA HA.
AH HA HA HA HA!!
I KNEW SHE WOULD DECEIVE US.
SO THAT'S IT!
WHAT A LAUGH. WHAT AN ABSOLUTE JOKESTER, MADAM EYE.
MADAM EYE SAID THAT TO GET EVEN MORE STRENGTH ...
AH... HA...
I WANTED TO BELIEVE IT...
...SHE NEEDED THE BLOOD OF THE DI MARIA FAMILY.
IT'S SO... FUNNY...

SO SHE WAS TRYING TO GET HER POWERS BACK... HILARI-OUS.
SHE CAN'T TURN BACK THE CLOCK ON HER SHRIVELED UP OLD SHELL, THOUGH.
...
BLOODY ...
... HUH?
BUT... I WAS WRONG.
MADAM EYE TOLD US THAT IF BLOODY'S ALIVE... WE'RE TO BRING HIM WITH US.
I THOUGHT IT WAS TO TAKE REVENGE ON HIM FOR BETRAYING HER.
MADAM EYE PLANS ON TAKING OVER BLOODY'S BODY.

THAT'S A PRETTY DANGEROUS TOPIC TO BRING UP.
Sway
SO SHE DIDN'T SIMPLY KIDNAP YZAK.
UNCLE... ARE YOU OKAY?
NO... I'M IN PRETTY BAD SHAPE.
Lend me a shoulder.
Koff!
ICHIRO.
WAKE UP YZAK RIGHT NOW.
I HEARD FROM LILY HOW TO DO IT.
HERE...?
TO BE HONEST, I'M NOT SURE WE CAN CARRY YZAK OUT OF HERE.
BUT IT'LL MAKE THINGS EASIER FOR US IF WE WAKE HIM UP HERE.

I AGREE.
I'LL PROTECT YOU FROM ANYTHING THAT SHOULD HAPPEN.
IF YOU GET THE POWER OF EXOR-CISM BACK...
...I HAVE A PLACE I HAVE TO GO.
I WON'T LET HER BE REVIVED.
I WON'T FORGIVE ANYONE WHO STANDS IN MY WAY.
I MUST HER FINISH OFF...
IN ORDER TO FULFILL MY "BLOOD PACT" WITH MARY---
...THAT ENDLESSLY OBSTRUC-TIVE WOMAN.
---I WILL ERADICATE MY OBSTRUCTIVE PAST.

---EVER SINCE I STARTED MY NEW LIFE AS A VAMPIRE.
IT'S AN URGE THAT OVER-TAKES ME FROM TIME TO TIME---
WHY---
BUT--- WHY IS IT---
WHEN I'M WASHED IN BLOOD ---
---IT MAKES ME CRAVE EVEN MORE BLOOD.
IT HAP-PENED --- AGAIN ---
WHEN-EVER I'M OUT---
---I CAN USUALLY HEAR HIM CRYING BY HIMSELF.
---CAN'T I HEAR HIS VOICE?

AND YET NOW... I HEAR NOTHING.
HEY.
CAN YOU HEAR... MY VOICE?
SAY SOME-THING.
COME ON... HEY...
WHY WON'T YOU ANSWER ME...
THERE'S NO POINT IF YOU WON'T COME OUT!
SAY SOME-THING!

THIS BODY BELONGS TO YOU.
BAM
DAMN IT!
OR... IS THIS YOUR WAY OF GIVING ME YOUR BODY?
THE FIRST IS THAT I BECOME A VAMPIRE.
TELL ME. WHAT WAS YOUR SECOND WISH?
THE SECOND ...
...IS THAT ONCE I AM A VAMPIRE, I MAKE MY BROTHER ONE.

SO YOU WANT TO TEST YOUR OWN BODY FIRST TO SEE IF YOU BOTH CAN BE VAMPIRES?
YOU SACRIFICED YOURSELF?
BUT FIRST I NEED TO BUILD A TOLERANCE TO BEING A VAMPIRE.
TURNING HIM INTO A VAMPIRE IS MY FIRST STEP TO LETTING HIM LIVE.
IF THERE'S A POSSIBILITY...
...I'M WILLING TO DO ANYTHING.

BLOOD ✦ 33 end

Bloody+Mary

BLOOD ✚ 34 Soul Fragment

I wonder if you caught that.

16 Years Ago
HEH HEH.
YUSEI. LOOK.
HE LOOKS JUST LIKE YOU WHEN YOU WERE A CHILD.

NO. THIS IS YOUR SON.
YOU MADE ANOTHER CLONE OF YOURSELF BESIDES ME?
HE WAS NAMED "ICHIRO."
MY... SON...?
MOTH-ER?
HE DOESN'T NEED HIS MOTHER.
SHE'D ONLY GET IN THE WAY.
WHERE'S... HIS MOTHER?

BUT I WAS SURPRISED A CLONE LIKE YOU HAD THE ABILITY TO PROCREATE.
YOU WENT AHEAD AND DID SOMETHING WITHOUT PERMIS-SION.
BUT I'M NOT MAD.
IN FACT, I'M HAPPY.
IT CAN'T BE...
THIS CHILD ALSO CARRIES THE BLOOD OF THE DI MARIA FAMILY.
HE'S GIFTED WITH THE POWER OF EXORCISM.
HE'S PRAC-TICALLY IMMORTAL.

THIS MADNESS...
BUT COULD IT BE BECAUSE HE HAS BOTHERSOME HUMAN BLOOD IN HIM?
I TRIED KILLING HIM, BUT HIS REGENERATIVE POWERS WERE SO SLOW.
YOU TESTED IT?
...CANNOT BE STOPPED ANYMORE.
BUT...
...THAT CHILD IS THE ONE THING I MUST PROTECT.
MASTER YZAK.
I HAVE A REQUEST.
PLEASE SEAL AWAY THAT CHILD'S POWER OF EXORCISM.
IT'S RARE FOR YOU TO ASK ME FOR SOMETHING.
WHAT IS IT?

IT WOULD BE BEST THAT HE KNEW NOTHING ABOUT THE POWER OF EXORCISM.
YOU HAVE ME.
I'M THE ONE WHO WILL LEAD YOU TO DEATH.
HIS POWER OF EXOR-CISM?
WHY DO THAT?
I WON'T LET THAT CHILD LEAD THE SAME LIFE I DO.
THERE'S NO GUARAN-TEE HE'LL BE OBEDIENT TO YOU.
WHAT IF HE DISOBEYS YOU AND KILLS THE LEGENDARY RED-HAIRED VAMPIRE?

I'LL WATCH OVER HIM AND RAISE HIM LIKE A NORMAL CHILD.
IF HE'S IMMORTAL, THEN I CAN'T KILL HIM.
NOR WILL I TELL HIM OF YOUR EXISTENCE.
squeeze
AND HE WILL NEVER KNOW THAT HE POSSESSES THE POWER OF EXORCISM.
THAT'S TRUE.
I SWEAR I WILL LEAD YOU TO THE PATH OF DEATH.
I WILL DIE FOR YOU.
YES... YUI.

WAIT FOR ME.
INDEED.
I BELIEVE YOUR WORDS, YUSEI.
"YZAK.
I SWEAR I'LL BE WITH YOU SOON.
"I'VE WAITED FOR YOU FOR SO LONG.

"While I was waiting for you...
"...I became this hideous thing."
"...WHY...?
"AND YET...
"WHY COULDN'T YOU COME SOONER...?"
YUI...?
DRIP

YUI!
Haah...
Haah...
Haah...

WE DID IT.
HE REALLY WOKE UP.
THANK GOD.
droop
haah...
haah...
I CAN'T GIVE... ANY MORE BLOOD ...
haah...
haah!...
YUI...
YUI...
haah...

QUICKLY!
TAKE ME DOWN THE PATH TO DEATH!
SHOW ME THE WAY TO YUI!
WHY!
AS LONG AS YOU'RE ALIVE, I CAN'T BE REUNITED WITH YUI!
WHY ARE YOU STILL ALIVE, YUSEI ?!

HURRY ...
HURRY ...
DIE FOR ME.
...!
KNOCK IT... OFF...
DON'T TOUCH ME WITH YOUR DIRTY HANDS !!

THUD
YOU'RE ...
... ICHIRO ?
YUSEI'S ALREADY ...
Hah hah...
OH... I GET IT NOW.
WHY ...?
Ahhahahah

WHY DID YOU PUT MY FATHER THROUGH ALL THAT?!
YOU COULD'VE EXPERI-MENTED ON YOURSELF, RATHER THAN ON HUMANS!
YOU'RE THE ONE WHO WANTS TO DIE!
WHAT'RE YOU SO MAD ABOUT?
YOU'RE A PRIEST, SO YOU SHOULD UNDER-STAND.
SUICIDE IS A SIN.

YOU THINK YOU'RE FREE OF SIN?
SINNERS CAN'T GO TO HEAVEN.
AND THEN I'D NEVER GET TO SEE YUI.
AND JUST WHAT SIN AM I GUILTY OF?
ME, WHO WAS CHOSEN BY GOD TO SERVE GOD.
chill
FORGET IT.
THERE'S NO POINT... TALKING TO YOU.

I CAN'T DO IT RIGHT NOW, BUT I WILL LEAD YOU TO YOUR DEATH.
TO MAKE THAT HAPPEN, PLEASE BREAK THE CURSE.
ICHIRO ...
AH, YES. OF COURSE.
COME HERE.

HE HAS MY FATHER'S VOICE.
HE SMELLS LIKE HIM TOO.

I CAN'T FORGIVE YZAK FOR MAKING MY FATHER SUFFER.
BUT...
BUT WHY DOES IT...
...FEEL SO GOOD IN HIS ARMS?
THERE. I'VE BROKEN THE CURSE.
NOW YOU CAN USE THE POWER OF EXOR-CISM.

THE ROSARIO'S SHAPE CHANGED.
YOU DID IT?
YES... I THINK SO.
THE ROSA-RIO...
...IS GUIDING ME.

I'M HAPPY FOR YOU, MARIA.
AT LAST YOU HAVE RECOVERED YOUR POWER OF EXORCISM.
NOW MY ROLE IS FULL-FILLED.
WHAT-EVER YOU DO, DON'T FORGET YOUR PROMISE.
I WILL CONTINUE TO THE NEXT PLACE.
AND ANOTHER THING... MARIA.

MY, OH MY, IT'S BEEN A LONG TIME.
WHY DID YOU BRING MASTER YZAK HERE?
He did get the Power of Exorcism back, right?!
WHIP
I TOLD YOU HE WAS COMING.
OH. IT'S YOU. YOU'VE COME BACK TO YOUR SENSES, THEN? WHAT A PITY.
SHALL I PUT THAT BACK ON YOU AGAIN?

N-NO THANKS... PLEASE DON'T INVOLVE ME ANY-MORE.
I EVEN HAD TO DRINK YOUR BLOOD.
I SEE. SO YOU'VE ALSO TASTED MY BLOOD.
THAT'S SO...
HEH HEH HEH ...
I KNEW IT! IS THERE SOME-THING IN IT ?!
Eep!
WHAT-EVER THE CASE, I'M JUST GLAD WE GOT HOME SAFE.
Though not exactly unscathed.

UNCLE.
I'M GOING OUT FOR A BIT.
NAH... I'M FINE.
Still a little faint, though.
Ow ow.
SHOULDN'T YOU BE RESTING?
YOU GAVE HIM A LOT OF YOUR BLOOD.
...
HOLD ON.
CAN'T THIS WAIT UNTIL MORNING?
YOU'RE GOING IN SEARCH OF MARY, AREN'T YOU?
I'M DIFFERENT THAN I'VE BEEN. YOU DON'T HAVE TO WORRY ABOUT ME.
I WANT TO TEST OUT MY POWER.

---LITTLE BY LITTLE.
UNCLE.
YOU'RE STARTING TO GET ME.
THERE'S SOMETHING ABOUT HIM...
ICHIRO SMILED.
---THAT'S---
---CHANGING---

Ah!
I SENSE A VAMPIRE AGAIN...
Haah...
Haah...
MARY... WHERE ARE YOU?

Haah...
Haah...
"MARY."
THUD
MARIA.
WHAT'RE YOU DOING WALKING AROUND OUT HERE BY YOURSELF?
YOU'VE ...
... RECOVERED YOUR POWER OF EXORCISM.

I WANT TO ASK YOU...
WHAT DID YOU WANT TO ACCOMPLISH BY RECOVERING MARY'S MEMORIES?
ME...?
OH. YOU'VE COME TO ASK ME TO KILL YZAK, RIGHT?
YUP.
AND I'VE BEEN LOOKING FOR YOU.
NO.
THAT'S NOT MY GOAL.
IT IS MY BUSINESS.
I TOLD YOU...
...THAT'S NONE OF YOUR BUSINESS.

I HURT MARY.
I...
...WANT TO APOLO-GIZE TO HIM.
WELL, WELL.
HAVE YOU CHANGED?
YOU'RE GENUINELY WORRIED ABOUT HIM?
I GUESS I CAN TELL YOU, IF THIS IS HOW YOU'RE GOING TO BE.

I'LL TELL HIM THE TRUTH.
SO THAT HE'LL STOP SAYING "I WANT TO DIE"...
...AND START SAYING "I WANT TO LIVE."
IT'S NOT LIKE I HATE HIM.
I JUST WANTED TO FREE HIM FROM THE SPELL.
sway
BUT...
...HE WON'T... COME OUT.
THE FACT THAT I ATTACKED YOU EARLIER ...
... PROVES IT'S TOO LATE FOR ME.
I NEED... BLOOD.

THE MORE BLOOD-STAINED MY HANDS BE-COME ...
...THE FAINTER HIS PRESENCE WITHIN ME BECOMES.
AND I CAN'T STOP IT!
SO... PLEASE ...
MARIA... I'M BEG-GING YOU.

KILL ME.
BEFORE I TAKE OVER THIS BODY COM-PLETELY ...
...WIPE OUT MY PRESENCE FROM INSIDE HIM.

BLOOD ✚ 34 end

This is sudden, but... Since there won't be any opportunity to showcase this later

Fluctuating Sadism Hierarchy!!

✧ Part I ✧

Bloody Mary

BLOOD ✚ 35 Atonement

"YOU'RE THE BIG BROTHER.
"NO MATTER WHAT HAPPENS, YOU MUST PROTECT THIS CHILD."
THAT'S RIGHT. AFTER MOTHER TOLD ME THAT, SHE SUDDENLY DISAP-PEARED.
THE TWO OF US WERE LEFT BEHIND.
THERE WAS NO ONE THERE TO LEND US A HAND.
I DIDN'T KNOW HOW WE'D SURVIVE.
WE REACHED THE END OF WHAT LITTLE REMAINING FOOD WE HAD IN THE HOUSE.

WE CAN'T STAY HERE. WE HAVE TO FIND SOME-PLACE NEW...
SO... HUNGRY ...
THE VILLAGE WAS SUFFER-ING FROM A DROUGHT SO THERE WAS A FOOD SHORT-AGE.
THERE WASN'T EVEN ANY FOOD TO STEAL.
BUT...
...I CAN'T GET VERY FAR WITH HIM.
IF I DIDN'T HAVE HIM...
...I COULD LEAVE HERE AS SOON AS I WANTED.
IF ONLY HE WEREN'T HERE.

MA...
RY...?
I
COULD
BE
FREE.
Perk
WHAT...
DID
I...
...AL-
MOST
...

---LET HAPPEN ---?
HE'S GONE.
WHY?
Huff!
WHERE DID HE GO?
Huff!
Rattle

MARY!
Haah...
Haah...
HERE.
YOU WERE CRYING YESTERDAY BECAUSE THE HUNGER WAS TOO MUCH FOR YOU, RIGHT?
BREAD ...?
I WENT TO A BUNCH OF HOMES ...
...AND GOT IT.
My fever broke.

I TRIED TO KILL...
I'M SORRY.
...MY ONE AND ONLY FAMILY.
I'M SORRY ...
THOSE ARE BRUISES FROM GETTING PUNCHED.
HERE. EAT.
HIS CLOTHES ARE COVERED IN MUD.
I'D WRITTEN HIM OFF AS A BURDEN ...
...AND WAS WISHING HE WAS GONE.
...THIS LIFE THAT I ALMOST TRIED TO SNUFF OUT WITH MY VERY OWN HANDS.
NO MATTER WHAT, I WILL PROTECT...
I'M SORRY.

I'LL SACRIFICE ANYTHING TO PROTECT IT.
KILL ME.
BEFORE I TAKE OVER THIS BODY COM-PLETELY ...
...WIPE OUT MY PRESENCE FROM INSIDE HIM.

NO.
I DON'T THINK MARY WOULD BE VERY HAPPY IF I EXOR-CISED YOU.

IF YOU DON'T GET RID OF ME, HE'LL DISAP-PEAR!
tap
slash

I WON'T KILL YOU.
WHAT'RE YOU...
BUT...
...I WANT TO TEST SOME-THING.
C'MERE.
DRINK.

WHAT...
...ARE YOU THINKING?
IF I DRINK BLOOD NOW, HE'LL DISAPPEAR EVEN MORE QUICKLY.
JUST DO IT.
IF YOU WANT MARY BACK, THEN DO AS I SAY.
Haah...
Haah...
NO... DAMN IT...
DON'T BOSS ME AROUND...
Haah...
Haah...
THE SMELL OF BLOOD IS DOWNRIGHT INTOXICATING.
OF ALL THE... GOD-DAMN...
I CAN'T STOP MYSELF.
tmb
WHY'RE YOU...
IT'S NO USE.

Hah...
MORE ---
MORE_
I CAN'T RESIST_

WAIT.
COULD YOU GO A LITTLE EASIER ON ME?
ANY MORE OF THIS... AND I'LL DIE.
YOU MADE ME DO IT.
HOLD... THIS.
WHAT'S THE DEAL?
I TOLD YOU.
I WANTED TO TEST SOME-THING.

HUH?
step
UNDER THE ONRUSH...
...OF THE SMELL OF BLOOD...
...THE VAMPIRES ARE GATHERING.
COME ON, MARY.
YOU TOLD ME SO YOURSELF.

THAT NO MATTER WHAT, YOU'LL PROTECT ME.
THAT AS LONG AS I KILL YOU, YOU'LL DO ANYTHING.
THEN REMEMBER.
MARY!!
THUMP
REMEMBER THE TASTE OF MY BLOOD.

REMEM-
BER
THE
TASTE
OF MY
BLOOD.

MARY...?
tmp

MARIA...

BLOODY HAS MADE A REAL MESS OF THINGS AGAIN.
AAAAW.
Haah...
HOW AM I SUPPOSED TO EXPLAIN THIS TO MADAM EYE?
WELL... IT'S STILL BETTER THAN THAT OTHER TIME.
100 YEARS AGO, WE COULDN'T EVEN FIND YZAK'S LOCATION IN THE FIRST PLACE.

WE'LL JUST HAVE TO CAPTURE HIM AGAIN.
WE KNOW WHERE HE IS.
OH ...?
YOU'RE AWFULLY CAREFREE ABOUT THIS.
THUNK

I'M REEEEALLY PISSED.
AND IT'S ALL THANKS TO YOUR BETRAYAL. ♥
BE-TRAYAL? WHAT'RE YOU TALKING ABOUT?
YANK
!
YOU KNEW THAT MADAM EYE WANTED TO REGAIN HER FORMER STRENGTH.
YOU KNEW, BUT YOU LIED TO US THIS ENTIRE TIME!

I QUIT.
I'M NOT ABOUT TO HAVE SOME DEFECT ORDER ME AROUND.
EITHER WAY, MADAM EYE IS DONE FOR.
THE VAMPIRE HYDRA HAS GONE TO KILL HER.
I DON'T CARE WHAT HAPPENS TO HER NOW—
Sr. it
BACK OFF!

DILA.
SHATTER!

ALDILA.
WHAT ARE YOU SO DESPERATE ABOUT?
MADAM EYE'S NOT EVEN STRONG.
SHE SHOULDN'T BE WORTH ANYTHING TO US.
Sorry for leaving you like that. ♡
CUTE LITTLE LADY.
WATCH YOURSELF ON THE STREETS AT NIGHT.
England, 300 Years Ago
UNSATISFYING.
NOTHING FILLS THE HOLE IN MY HEART.

I LIKE HEARING THE AGONY OF HUMANS AS I SUCK THEIR BLOOD.
TO ME, DRINKING BLOOD ISN'T ABOUT A MEAL. I JUST DO IT FOR FUN.
RECKLESSLY ATTACKING HUMANS AGAIN...
I GUESS YOU COULD CALL IT BLOOD LUST?
LIKE THAT.
YOU'RE NOT EVEN HUNGRY, SO WHAT PLEASURE DO YOU FIND?
...NO MATTER HOW MANY PEOPLE I KILL...
...IT'S STILL NO FUN AT ALL.
IT'S UGLY AND I DON'T UNDERSTAND IT.
HOW VULGAR.
BUT ANYWAY, WHY IS IT...
I DON'T NEED YOU TO UNDERSTAND IT.

glint
HM?
DIE!
ALDILA!
flap

YOU HURT MY FACE... I'LL KILL YOU FOR THAT.
RIGHT BACK AT YOU.
Hisssss!
STOP IT.
It's unbecoming.
YOU NEVER GROW TIRED OF IT AFTER ALL THESE CENTURIES?
DON'T ACT LIKE YOU'RE ABOVE BEING CURIOUS.
YOU CURSED GENTLEMAN!
WE COULD KILL EACH OTHER UNTIL THE END OF TIME AND NEVER SETTLE ANYTHING.
WHAT FUN IS THERE IN A WAR WHERE THERE'S NO VICTORY OR DEFEAT?

IT'S NOT ABOUT IT BEING FUN OR NOT.
BUT THERE'S NO STRONGER VAMPIRE THAN US OUT THERE.
AND IT'S BORING!
BORING!!
WE WERE BORED.
WOULD THIS BOREDOM CONTINUE AS LONG AS WE LIVED?
IN ORDER TO END IT, OUR ONLY CHOICE WAS TO KILL OURSELVES.
THAT REMINDS ME.
I HEARD A RUMOR TODAY THAT CAUGHT MY ATTENTION.
RUMOR?
FAR TO THE SOUTH FROM HERE IS A RED-HAIRED VAMPIRE.

A RED-HAIRED VAM-PIRE...
SO YOU MEAN SOMEONE COMMITTED THE TABOO?
DON'T YOU THINK YOU'D LIKE TO BATTLE THEM TO THE DEATH?
MIGHT BEAT BEING BORED.
WE WOULD COME TO KNOW---
---OUR OWN AMBI-TIONS.
OUR OWN WEAK-NESSES.
OUR OWN WRETCHED-NESS.

WHAT... IS THIS?
...
NO... WAY.
Kah...
ON THAT DAY ---
---WHEN I MET YOU.

AAAW, WHAT A BORE.
THERE'S SO MANY OF YOU, AND YOU STILL CAN'T EVEN HURT ME.
BUT...
I SUPPOSE YOU THREE ARE ON THE STRONGER SIDE?
Hee
I'M A LITTLE SUR-PRISED.
hee
LISTEN, BOYS... IF YOU WORK FOR ME, I'LL LET YOU LIVE. OKAY?
TO THINK THERE ARE VAMPIRES WHO DON'T IMMEDIATELY DIE AFTER BATTLING ME.

OR...
...YOU'LL DIE RIGHT HERE AND NOW.
OOOH.
I FINALLY MET HER.
WE LOST EVERYTHING THAT DAY.

AFTER THAT DAY...
SHE'S ALWAYS FLYING OFF SOME-WHERE.
...I LOST TRACK OF TIME.
rustle
HUH? WHERE'D SHE GO?
MADAM EYE.

DID SOME-THING HAPPEN ?
HE'S WORRIED ABOUT YOU.
HE'S VERY ATTACHED TO YOU, MADAM EYE.
IT'S YOU. ALDILA.
I DON'T NEED YOUR WORRY.
LEAVE ME BE.
WHAT?
I MEAN ...
MADAM EYE, ARE YOU HIDING SOME-THING?

LOOK.
YOU NEVER USED TO LET ME TOUCH YOU SO READILY.
AT THAT MOMENT, I CONFIRMED IT.

DON'T WORRY.
IF YOU DON'T WANT THE OTHERS TO KNOW, I WON'T SAY A WORD.
BUT...
...FOR SOME REASON...
NOT TO VESPA OR CARDINAL.
...IT WAS SO ENDEARING.
THE HOLE IN MY HEART ...
...IS FILL-ING UP.
IT'LL BE OUR LITTLE SECRET.
I WANT TO DEVOTE EVERYTHING TO THIS PERSON.

THAT'S THE GIST OF IT. IT'S SO MESSED UP.
SO YOU'RE SAYING...
...YOU AND I WERE DECEIVED BY DILA AND MADAM EYE?
Huh?
WHY?
WE HAVE TO GO AFTER HIM.
DILA'S THE ONLY ONE WHO KNOWS WHERE MADAM EYE IS.
I CAN'T BELIEVE IT.
TO THINK THAT THE MADAM EYE WHO POSSESSED THAT BEAUTIFUL AND PERFECT STRENGTH IS GONE.

I TASTED MARIA'S BLOOD.
A RAY OF LIGHT SHINED THROUGH THE DARKNESS.
THAT'S RIGHT... I HAVE TO PROTECT MARIA.
THE LIGHT I WISHED FOR IS IN THAT LIGHT.
THE REASON FOR ME TO PROTECT MARIA.
MARIA...
WHAT I WANT MORE THAN ANYTHING ELSE.
MARIA...
SLUMP
HELP ME...
ONLY MARIA CAN GRANT THAT FOR ME.

I... WANT TO DIE...
I WANT TO RUN AWAY.
IT'S FINE.
I'LL KILL YOU.
IF I JUST DIE—
I WANT TO DIE.
IT'S ALL MY FAULT.
I WANT TO DIE.
I WANT TO DIE.
I KILLED HIM.
WHAT'S UP WITH HIM?
HE'S BACK ---
--- BUT ---
---WHAT SHOULD I DO?
WHAT SHOULD I DO?

I'M SORRY.
MARY, I'M SORRY.
WHY... ARE YOU APOLO-GIZING, MARIA?
AFTER ALL, MARIA.
YOU'RE GOING TO KILL ME, RIGHT?

THAT ---
---IS THE ONE PROMISE BETWEEN MARY AND ME.
IT'S OKAY.
"SO THAT HE'D STOP SAYING 'I WANT TO DIE'...
"...AND START SAYING 'I WANT TO LIVE.'"
THAT'S RIGHT.
ALL I CAN DO FOR YOU IS KILL YOU.
I'LL MAKE YOUR WISH COME TRUE.

BLOOD + 35 end

This is sudden, but... Since there won't be any opportunity to showcase this later

Fluctuating Sadism Hierarchy!!

✧ Part II ✧

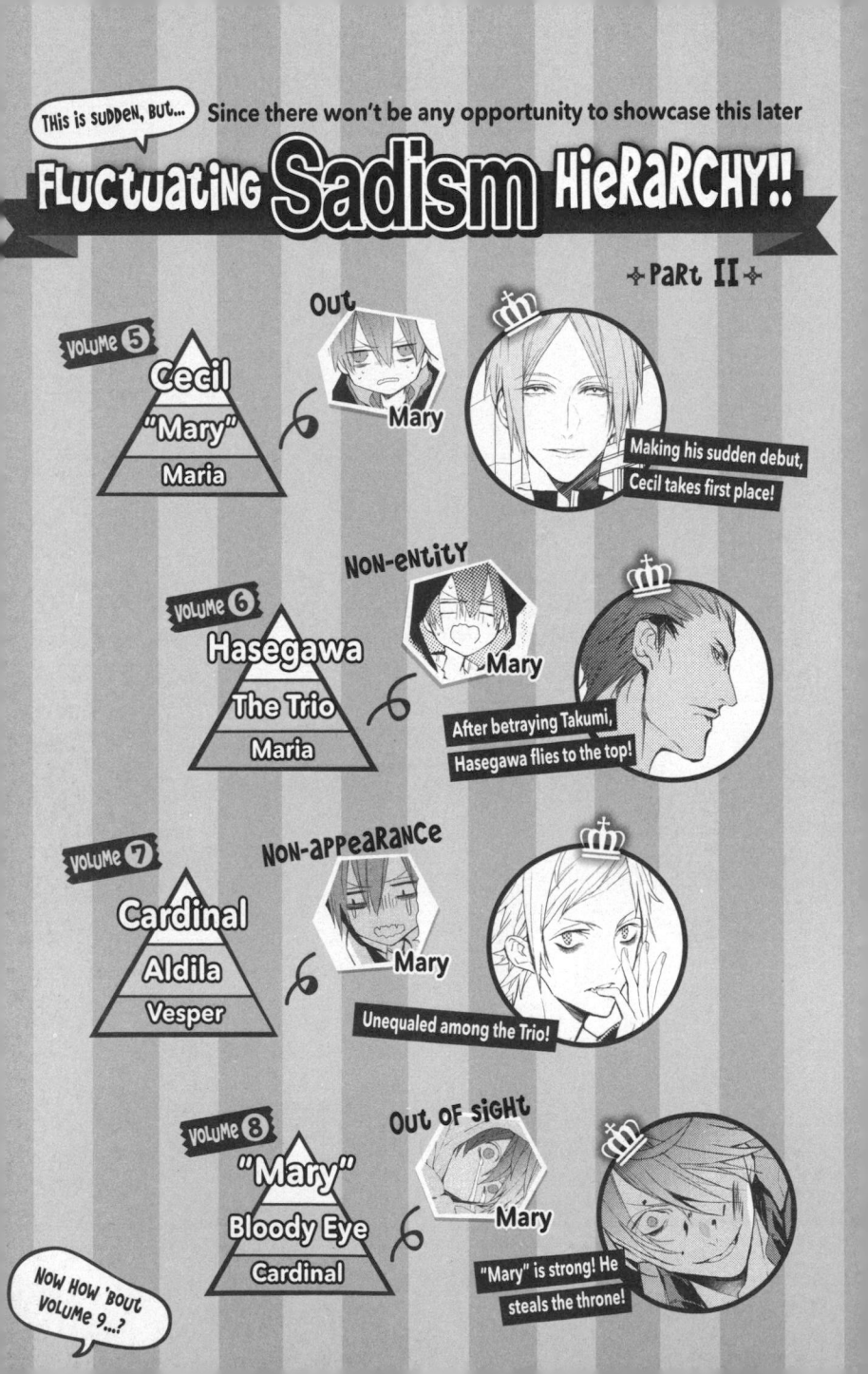

Bloody Mary

I PROMISED YOU.
IT'S OKAY.
I'LL MAKE YOUR WISH COME TRUE.
I'LL PUT A STOP...
BUT...
...TO ALL YOUR FEAR AND SUFFERING.
HEAR MY ONE LAST REQUEST.
I SWEAR I'LL KILL YOU.
IF YOU WISH FOR DEATH WITH ALL YOUR HEART.

RE::QUEST?
I'LL... DO ANYTHING.
IF IT MEANS I CAN DIE...
...I'LL DO ANY-THING. SO PLEASE ...
KILL ME.
OKAY, THEN.
FACE "MARY" INSIDE YOU.

STOP RUNNING FROM "MARY"...
...AND FACE THE TRUTH.
IF YOU CAN DO THAT...
ALL I CAN DO FOR YOU IS KILL YOU.
SO...

THE ONLY ONE WHO CAN SAVE YOU...
...I'LL PLACE ALL MY HOPES...
...IS "MARY."
...THEN I'LL KILL YOU.
...IN MY FINAL REQUEST.

IT'LL BE OKAY.
DON'T BE AFRAID.
AND WITH THAT...
I'LL BE WAIT-ING.
THIS... IS MY FINAL REQUEST.
I'LL GRANT YOU YOUR HEART'S GREATEST WISH.

IF MARY IS ABLE TO WISH TO LIVE...
...THE MOMENT HE STARTS WANTING TO LIVE...
...I AND MY POWERS OF EXOR-CISM...
...WILL BECOME A THREAT TO MARY.
WHEN THAT TIME COMES ...
...YOU DON'T HAVE TO COME BACK TO ME.
I WILL FREE YOU FROM ME.
IT'S SO STRANGE.
THAT DAY ...

WHEN I FIRST MET YOU, I NEVER DREAMED ---
---THAT I'D WANT YOU TO WANT TO LIVE.
AND SO THIS ---
---IS HOW IT MUST BE---
GOOD-BYE.
MARY.

I HAVE TO...
... FACE ... "MARY" ?
NO.
I CAN'T...
BECAUSE... MARY'S...

MARY!
stagger
I... HAVE TO HELP ...
I HAVE TO...
... HELP MARY ...
... QUICKLY ...!!
Haah...
Haah...

rumble
WHERE'S MARY?
YOU'RE ALL SO PERSIS-TENT...
...ONE AFTER THE OTHER.
WHAT THE... HECK?
A VAMPIRE'S CORPSE?
TO WHERE HE IS.
I'VE GOT TO...
... HURRY BACK...

"I HATE YOU, MARY!"
plip
THAT'S RIGHT.
I BETRAYED YOU.
I LEFT YOU ALL ALONE.
I DON'T MIND IF YOU HATE ME.
SO LONG ---
SSSSHH
--- AS YOU CAN LIVE.
Haah
Haah
MARY!
MARY!
MARY ...

!
NOW'S NOT THE TIME FOR ---
--- A RELAPSE.
IT HURTS ---
IT HURTS SO MUCH!
Koff!
Koff!
Koff!
I HAVE TO FIND --- MARY QUICKLY ---
Huff...
Huff...
IF I DON'T --- I'LL...
HUH ...?

Ah...
WHAT WAS THAT... JUST NOW ...?
HE'S ...
THAT WOULD BE...
Hoah
Hoah
splash
I'VE GOT A BAD FEEL-ING.
splash

---THE WORST SCENARIO.
WHY ...?
WHY NOW...

AH!
!
HE'S STILL BREATHING.
THERE'S STILL TIME.
BUT...
I DON'T HAVE ENOUGH TIME TO BRING HIM TO HYDRA.
IN THAT CASE ...
I'LL...
...MAKE YOU...

...A VAMPIRE.

HYDRA.
NOW THAT I'M A VAMPIRE ...
...CAN I MAKE HIM A VAMPIRE?

IF YOU'RE THINKING OF TESTING IT OUT, DON'T.
THERE'S NO TELLING WHAT MIGHT HAPPEN.

I DON'T KNOW. I'VE NEVER HEARD OF THAT BEING DONE BEFORE.

BUT ...

THERE'S A CHANCE YOU COULD DIE.
... MARY ?
YOU SAID YOU'D BE BACK ...
... BEFORE DAY-BREAK.

NO!
I WON'T LET YOU TURN TO ASH!
NO ...
UUH ...

MARY?!
MA–
THIS IS ALL ...
DON'T TOUCH HIM!
THIS IS ALL YOUR FAULT!

HUH?
DON'T YOU... KNOW ANY-THING?!
THE REASON MARY BECAME A VAMPIRE...
...WHY HE WAS WILLING TO SACRIFICE HIMSELF WAS TO MAKE YOU A VAMPIRE TOO.
SACRIFICE---?
WHAT---
---IS SHE TALKING ABOUT?
ALL OF IT WAS TO LET YOU LIVE.
MARY SACRIFICED HIMSELF FOR YOU.

IT'S BECAUSE OF YOU THAT MARY'S DEAD!
YOUR VERY EXIS-TENCE ...
... KILLED MARY!

BUT...
MARY...
...DIED.
HE DIED...
...BECAUSE OF ME.
WHY... DIDN'T I REALIZE?
WHY... DID I THINK... MARY HATED ME...
...
THAT HE HATED...
...
THAT...
...WAS HIS FINAL DAY.
THAT'S RIGHT.
I STILL HAVEN'T TOLD MARY.

I'M SCARED.
I'M SCARED, MARIA.
THERE'S SOMETHING I NEED TO TELL HIM BEFORE I DIE.
WHILE HE'S STILL INSIDE ME.
"IT'LL BE OKAY."
"DON'T BE AFRAID."
MAR...Y...
"I'LL ALWAYS BE WITH YOU."
MARY.
"YOU BECOME ME."
MARY...
YOU LIVED JUST FOR MY SAKE.

I DON'T NEED YOU TO FORGIVE ME.
MARY!
MARY!
I DIDN'T MEAN WHAT I SAID ABOUT HATING YOU.
MARY!
QUIT REPEATING YOURSELF. IT'S GETTING ANNOYING.
I CAN HEAR YOU.
YOU MEAN MORE TO ME THAN ANYBODY!

JUST KIDDING.
KEEP YELLING.
YOU FINALLY... CALLED FOR ME.

WHO'RE YOU?
ARE YOU A BAD GUY WHO CAME IN THROUGH THE WINDOW?
MAYBE.
EVERY-ONE'S AFRAID OF ME.
I DON'T MIND BAD GUYS.
HEY, IF IT'S OKAY WITH YOU, WILL YOU PLAY WITH ME?
THERE ARE PLENTY OF BAD GUYS ALREADY IN THIS CASTLE.
I GET SO LONELY ALL BY MYSELF AT NIGHT.
IT'S THANKS TO THEM THAT SO MUCH CAN GET DONE.

I'M SURE WE'LL BECOME THE BEST OF FRIENDS.
LONG TIME NO SEE, BLOODY EYE.
HYDRA...

MEETING YOU LIKE THIS...
...REMINDS ME OF THE FIRST DAY WE MET.
THOUGH THE CASTLE YOU LIVED IN WAS COMPLETELY DIFFERENT.
TO THINK YOU HAVE TO HIDE YOURSELF AWAY IN THIS DECREPIT OLD PLACE NOW.
HOW SAD.
IT WAS QUITE A FEAT TRACKING DOWN YOUR LOCATION.
BUT...
I'M IMPRESSED ...

...WITH HOW YOU STILL CLING TO POWER IN YOUR WRETCHED-NESS...
...EVEN IF IT'S REDUCED YOU TO SUCH A SORRY STATE.

WHY HAVE YOU COME, HYDRA?
BUT...
I NEVER PLANNED TO INTERFERE WITH YOU AGAIN.
...YOUR PLAN...
...IS A BIT OF AN EYE-SORE FOR ME.
AND SO...
...I'VE COME TO DISPOSE OF...
...THE DEFECT I HELPED CREATE.

CLANG
SWISH
DON'T MAKE ME LAUGH, HYDRA.
!
grrk
grrk
SHE STILL HAS ENOUGH POWER TO RESIST ME?!

YOU SAY YOU DIDN'T HAVE PLANS TO INTER-FERE?
I KNOW YOU WERE ONLY AFRAID OF ME AND WERE RUNNING AWAY.
SO YOU STILL HAVE TIME FOR JOKES?
DASH
...IS UP!
BUT THAT TIME ...

SLASH
DIS-GRACEFUL.

WHOOSH!
IT ENDS NOW.
smirk
MADAM EYE!

MADE... IT...

SLOSH
slide
Hah...
OH... ALDILA.
YOU REALLY ARE A FOOLISH MAN.
MADAM EYE.
TAKE ...
...MY BLOOD ... USE IT...

EVER SINCE WE MET...
...YOU'VE BEEN BEGGING ME.
BEGGING ME TO RULE YOU.
I SEE...
THEN I'LL GRANT YOU...
...YOUR WISH.
AS A REWARD.
YOU MAY DIE FOR ME.

MADAM EYE...
GOOD-BYE.
I'M BEING FILLED.
BECOM-ING YOUR BLOOD.
BECOM-ING YOUR FLESH.
BECOM-ING A PART OF YOU.
EVEN IF IT'S ONLY FOR A LITTLE WHILE.

I LOVE YOU.
LOVE ...?
YOU WOULD SPEAK THAT WORTHLESS WORD TO ME EVEN IN YOUR LAST HOUR?
RIGHT ... HYDRA?
YOU WERE FIXATED ON LOVE TOO.
YOU TRUSTED ME, LOVED ME AND MADE ME A VAMPIRE.
YOU MUST'VE BEEN DEVAS-TATED TO BE BETRAYED BY ME.

SO YOU MADE A NEW VAMPIRE ...
...HOPING TO CREATE A SUBSTITUTE FOR ME.
NO.
DID IT DISTRACT YOU FROM THE LONELINESS?
DID YOU GET THAT LOVE THAT YOU WANTED SO BADLY?
NOT TRUE.
I DID FIND TRUE LOVE.
MARY WASN'T A SUBSTITUTE FOR YOU.
Heh!
YOU HAVEN'T CHANGED AT ALL, HYDRA.
AND TO MAKE THAT LOVE EVERLASTING ...
...I'M GOING TO FULFILL MY PROMISE.
THEN ...
...WHY?

WHY ARE YOU CRYING?
POOR HYDRA.
SO YOU FINALLY REALIZE.
NOBODY LOVES YOU.
YOU CAN NEVER BE LOVED.

BLOOD ✦ 36 end

Bloody Mary

A Colloquy on the Bedroom: Follow-Up

AND IT'S EVEN WORSE THAN THE PREVIOUS DAY.

Thank you very much for picking up volume 9 of *Bloody Mary*!
You may have noticed the release of volume 9 is exactly three years after the start of the serialization.
It's thanks to your support throughout all this time.
Thank you so much.
Bloody Mary will be reaching the climax of the story soon.
I hope you watch over the characters for the little remaining time we have left with them!

SPECIAL THANKS

Mihoru / M-fuchi / H-gawa / T-mizu-sama / T-ko-sama

Production Team/Support
Haruo / Sumida / M-ika

Editor S / Designer
Everyone involved /
And everyone who read this

Aldila

POINT OF PRIDE:
His eye. When he thinks about how a part of his body is always with Mistress Eye, he is endlessly excited.

Vesper

POINT OF PREFERENCE:
His glasses. He got them when glasses with temples first became standard. Since then, he's considered them a part of his face.

Cardinal

POINT THAT'S NONNEGOTIABLE:
Overly long sleeves. When Aldila tried to copy his style, he put a stop to it.

Announcement of Voting Results!! Announcement of Voting Results!!

Announcement of Voting Results!! Announcement of Voting Results!!

nal

Rosario di Maria

Yuki

Bloody Mary

Akaza Samamiya

akaza samamiya

Born November 7, Scorpio, blood type B.
I got a customized pillow made, and I
sleep even more soundly than before.

Bloody Mary

Volume 9
Shojo Beat Edition

story and art by Akaza Samamiya

translation Katherine Schilling
touch-up art & lettering Sabrina Heep
design Shawn Carrico
editor Erica Yee

BLOODY MARY Volume 9
© Akaza SAMAMIYA 2016
First published in Japan in 2016 by KADOKAWA CORPORATION, Tokyo.
English translation rights arranged with KADOKAWA CORPORATION, Tokyo.

The stories, characters and incidents mentioned in this publication are entirely fictional.

No portion of this book may be reproduced or transmitted in any form or by any means without written permission from the copyright holders.

Printed in the U.S.A.

Published by VIZ Media, LLC
P.O. Box 77010
San Francisco, CA 94107

10 9 8 7 6 5 4 3 2 1
First printing, December 2017

www.viz.com

www.shojobeat.com

6

stop

YOU MAY BE READING THE

wrong way

IT'S TRUE: In keeping with the original Japanese comic format, this book reads from right to left—so action, sound effects and word balloons are completely reversed. This preserves the orientation of the original artwork—plus, it's fun! Check out the diagram shown here to get the hang of things, and then turn to the other side of the book to get started!

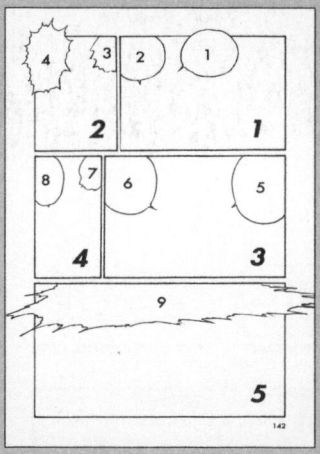